Climb up the Tree
with
Zacchaeus

AN ACTION RHYME BOOK

Climb up the Tree
with
Zacchaeus

Leena Lane and Chris Saunderson

Pretend to count coins

Money! Money!
Count the taxes!
Count the taxes, with Zacchaeus!

Look sad and wipe eyes

Sad! Sad!
He has no friends.
No one is friends with Zacchaeus.

Cup hand round ear

Listen! Listen!
Jesus is coming!
Hurry to watch, with Zacchaeus!

Stretch on tiptoes with hand above eyes

Stretch! Stretch!
Too small to see!
No one's as small as Zacchaeus.

Climb a tree with hands and feet

Climb! Climb!
Climb up the tree.
Reach the top branches, Zacchaeus!

Look! Look!
Jesus is coming!
Look over the crowds, with Zacchaeus!

Point to the distance

Come down! Come down!
Jesus is calling!
Jesus is calling, to Zacchaeus!

Beckon with hands

Stretch up high, then move hands downwards

Climb! Climb!
Back down the tree,
Carefully down, with Zacchaeus.

Pour out a drink and offer it

Home! Home!
Take Jesus home.
Jesus will eat, with Zacchaeus!

Mutter... Mutter...
People are cross.
Why is he going with Zacchaeus?

Whisper behind a hand, looking cross

Give! Give!
He'll give all he has.
Share out the money with Zacchaeus!

Offer with outstretched hands

Smile and clap hands

Hooray! Hooray!
Jesus is pleased.
Jesus is pleased, with Zacchaeus.

Published in the UK by Scripture Union

207-209 Queensway, Bletchley,

Milton Keynes, Bucks MK2 2EB

ISBN 1 84427 094 7

First edition 2005

Copyright © AD Publishing Services Ltd

1 Churchgates, The Wilderness,

Berkhamsted, Herts HP4 2UB

Text copyright © 2005 AD Publishing Ltd, Leena Lane

Illustrations copyright © 2005 Chris Saunderson

Editorial Director Annette Reynolds

Art Director Gerald Rogers

Pre-production Krystyna Hewitt

Production John Laister

Printed and bound in China